Slipping
on a
Banana

Dave Rochford

AuthorHouse™ UK
1663 Liberty Drive
Bloomington, IN 47403 USA
www.authorhouse.co.uk
UK TFN: 0800 0148641 (Toll Free inside the UK)
UK Local: 02036 956322 (+44 20 3695 6322 from outside the UK)

This book is printed on acid-free paper.

ISBN: 978-1-6655-9779-1 (sc)
ISBN: 978-1-6655-9778-4 (e)

Print information available on the last page.

Published by AuthorHouse 03/24/2022

authorHOUSE®

This book is an adventure. A true-life account of a young consultant who upon leaving University spent two years in Dominica in the West Indies attached to the Government as an Economist. He experienced many bizarre events such as Juve/carnival, discovering strangely planted plantations, stowing away on a banana boat, near drowning at sea, and pretending to run the island for a couple of days.

He also witnessed a civil revolution and overthrow of the then Prime Minister, the celebration of independence from Great Britain, and the ravages of Hurricane David, which are stories to be told in their own right.

Overall, a good holiday read, interesting, funny at times, thoughtful and hopefully inspirational.

Enjoy!

I dedicate this book to the government and people of Dominica, to the Overseas Development Institute, the Rockefeller Foundation and British Overseas Development Administration, who gave me the opportunity to work in the beautiful island of Dominica, WI.

I also dedicate this book to all the friends and acquaintances that I made and especially to my wife Anne who supported me in Dominica and put up with me for many years, as well as my children who had to read, grin and bear it.

Table of Contents

Introduction

A lot happened in the two years I spent in Dominica and whilst it occurred some 40 years ago the story has taken years to unfold and be told, but told it must be, yes told, as much of it is incredible, if not unbelievable, funny and sometimes serious, but also interesting and enjoyable.

Background

History

Dominica, not to be confused with the Dominican Republic, is 35 miles long and up to 10 miles wide, and lies between the French Islands of Martinique and Guadeloupe in the centre of the Windward Isles in the Eastern Caribbean. It became independent from Britain whilst I was there in 1978.

The island whilst still largely devoid of tourism is truly a tropical paradise, with steep volcanic mountains and sea shelves, and endless long sweeping palm fronted beaches. It also possesses the second largest boiling lake in the World, hot springs, luscious rich vegetation and allegedly 365 rivers, one for each day of the year!

It also contains the last remaining tribe of Caribs living in a vast reserve on the eastern side of the island. Carib derives from the word Cannibal, and the Caribs originated from Brazil. They were forced north by the Walongs, a fierce warring tribe and eventually found their way to Dominica. Caribs have very distinctive and unusual looks, honed slim but shapely bodies, oriental eyes and mulato coloured skin. Interestingly as Cannibals, they used to stuff their prey, especially white Europeans, with peppers and spices to improve the taste.

After early Arawak settlement, the Caribs invaded and ousted the Arawaks in the 1300's. The fierce resistance of the Carib people and the lack of any rumour of gold on the island kept the Spanish from attempting a settlement.

The French and English became interested in Dominica in the 1600's, but they left it to the Caribs and both agreed by treaty not to settle it. In the 1700's, however both sides made "timber raids" on the island to harvest its rich store of lumber. Beginning in 1690, and at an accelerated pace after 1715, France began to colonize Dominica.

In 1761, the English conquered Dominica as part of the Seven Years' War. The French made several attempts to retake it but never could.

In the past, the island often changed hands between the British and the French, resulting from concessions made on the outcome of wars and battles between them, and in 1801, as a consequence of losing the Battle of Waterloo, the French finally conceded the island to the British.

Following the changes in ownership, monks from both nations attempted to convert the Caribs to Christianity, but invariably ended up on the spit!

In addition, because of different ownership, the language evolved as Patio (pronounced "patwa") – a mixture of pigeon English and French.

Finally, in 1961, an independence movement arose in Dominica. In 1968, the island gained self-rule within the British Empire, and on 3 November 1978, gained full autonomy.

Economy

From an economic standpoint, the island depends mainly on the sale of bananas, which are subsidized by the European Economic Union. The island has a population of approximately 72000 and GDP per capita per annum of about $6500. Over 99% of the population is West Indian, and the rest are white Caucasian i.e., less than 750 in number.

A small and mountainous island in the Lesser Antilles, Dominica is a member of the Organization of Eastern Caribbean States (OECS). Prime Minister Roosevelt Skerrit of the Dominica Labour Party has been in office since 2004. Historically, the economy has depended on agriculture (again bananas) and tourism.

The government's efforts to promote diversification have led to creation of an offshore medical education sector and have encouraged investments in such agricultural exports as coffee, patchouli, aloe vera, exotic fruits, and cut flowers.

Devastation from Hurricane Maria, which destroyed much of the country's agricultural sector and damaged its transportation and physical infrastructure in 2017, has stressed the government's already fragile finances.

Whilst it has always been an island of beauty with volcanic mountains, tropical rain forests, and beaches, producing as a result, rich fertile soils, its rugged terrain has nonetheless restricted the development of needed infrastructure such as roads making expansion of agro-industry and transport of people and goods difficult. However, with the growth in world environmental concern and appreciation of green natural habitats there has and will be continued growth in eco-tourism.

Bio-Diversity

Dominica, by its volcanic nature is very mountainous. Whilst being a relatively small island (35 miles by 10 miles), it nonetheless contains many rivers (one for each day of the year) and three hundred miles of hiking paths. Additionally, 20 percent of the land is designated as a national park and two-thirds of the island is rainforest

Setting Off

I applied for an ODI two-year fellowship whilst at Manchester University doing a Master's Degree in Economics but missed the application date and whist waiting a year to apply again I worked In the Head Office of Vesties. Union International, a meat and dairy company based in Smithfield's meat market in London.

The market is certainly not the place for teetotal vegans, as I can still smell the blood and beer today for when I went into work I often had to sidestep pig heads and hindquarters thrown across the pavement into the basement stores as well as manoeuvre around swarms of market porters staggering from pubs after they had finished the night shift and force-fed themselves on beer and bacon butties.

So how did the market boy become a management consultant? Well, it was not an easy transition. At interview with a dozen or so highbrow economists from the Overseas Development Institute, I was initially disappointed to find that I was placed on a reserve list of candidates but then to my surprise I was awarded a fellowship with the Ministry of Agriculture in Dominica. Of course, at the time I did not have a clue where it was and what I would be doing.

I later found out that Mr Castor, the Permanent Secretary from the Ministry, selected me because I had been a taxi driver during summer vacation at University. Again, at the time it did make me think that perhaps the Permanent Secretary may have just lost a driver!

The fellowship was also offered as a married posting and having known my partner since school I decided to bite the bullet that her mother would have fired had we gone together and not got married. I jokingly referred to her ever since as Ma Hitler though a surprising combination of Margaret Thatcher and Sister Theresa would perhaps be more appropriate.

Anyway,we had little time before departing to the West Indies so all preparations and the stag/hen parties and wedding were all rushed resulting in a variety of cock-ups. For example, the strippers didn't turn up to my stag party and my grandfather had to keep changing his glasses as the strippers were replaced by old black and white faded naughty videos.

I referred to my sister as my daughter in my wedding and my father had to receive medical attention as his new Portuguese partner lacked attention but with a strong Latino temperament managed to place her stiletto shoe in his head.

Ma Hitler (mother-in-law) was not happy either as my friends drank all the beer in the party that followed over the following two days.

Honeymoon in Barbados

On the third day after the wedding, my wife and I departed to Barbados for a briefing by the regional office of the British Overseas Development Authority (ODA). In reality, this was also to be our honeymoon lasting all of three days. ODA were very obliging but not more so than my wife. I do not think I could have lasted any longer as it rained continuously and most of the time was spent in the bedroom. Evidently, the island is very beautiful but I decided that duty should come first.

On the odd occasion, we wandered from the bedroom and hotel we would walk along the beach even when it was raining, as it tended to be light, warm, and still considered to be paradise compared to the usual vagaries of the weather in the UK.

We also travelled around the island by rental car, through sugar cane plantations, small villages and coastal resorts. It was all very flat. We also visited the east side of the island, which was subject to more rough waves and beaches. Less developed at the time but ideal as a surfer's paradise.

One night we ventured into downtown Bridgetown and hit a Jazz Club. It was reminiscent of a 1930s film set in a New Orleans sweat club, very hot, smoky and heaving with bodies of all shapes and colour gyrating to the rhythm and blues. You could not help fall into the swing of it and before long it was the early hours and we were heading home to the hotel to sleep it off.

Next day at breakfast, well breakfast at lunchtime, I was surprisingly talking to my new wife about politics in the Caribbean (the sort of thing one does on a honeymoon or in an episode of "Two and a Half Men") when an English grey-haired gentleman sporting a checked tie-n-jacket and white flannels leaned over from a neighbouring table. He then went on to tell me to be quiet in case I was overheard.

I looked around and besides him, there was no one there. I wondered if I had been followed since my meeting with British government or perhaps being tested for MI5 material. Very odd and seemingly very unlikely. I just said "Sure", turned back and tucked into my breakfast.

Landing in Dominica

We then flew into Dominica on the airline LIAT (known locally as "Leave Island Any Time" or "Lost In-between Antigua and Trinidad" a reputation duly deserved even though the Caribbean islands were very close to each other so as soon as you took off you were landing.

However, the approach to the airport In Dominica at that time was one of the scariest you could encounter. As you flew off the sea towards a mountain wandering if the pilot was on a suicide mission, the plane would then bank steeply and you would think the pilot has chickened out, and then as the plane dives towards the earth then levels out and squeezes between coconut trees, you think he has lost his mind again. Then you wander if he was ever a low flying acrobatic pilot who also loved salty coconuts as the plane appears to collect them whist kissing the trees and hurtling down the narrow short runway that runs quickly back to the sea.

If that wasn't enough on debarking you were directed through a wooden shack (called Customs) and met by a rust bucket on wheels (called a taxi) and whilst the journey from the Airport to Roseau - the capital on the other side of the island --is only twenty miles, the journey took over two hours. The road, which would often be confused with a river, would twist between steep mountains and valleys, landslides and potholes, and whilst beautiful it was difficult to appreciate as you hung on for dear life.

When eventually we had traversed the mountains and hit some flat land I noticed estates of trees with small green fruit, which I didn't recognise. The taxi driver informed me that they were limes. Then over the local radio, there was an announcement that an Agricultural Expert had just arrived and little did I know that later I would be leading a review of the lime industry. I felt like Mr Bean – a total idiot!

Getting Settled

On arriving in Roseau, the capital, we were booked into the Fort Young Hotel located on the coast and overlooking the port and approaches to the town. We stayed there for six weeks in what seemed an enchanting and historic fortress but with posh furnishings, tropical food, cocktails and all the trimmings.

We tried every type of food and drink. The fruit was larger than life, rum cocktails were a dream, and occasionally we went to the extreme such as eating conch - giant sea slugs - that fortunately tended to go straight through you and take everything else with it, Equally there were deceptively attractive large spiked exotic fruits such as Dorian - a large white horned fruit that when opened smelled worse than a blocked toilet in a crowded music festival.

Clearly, some bowel adjustment and acclimatisation was required.

Moving on, so to speak, for permanent accommodation we eventually found a furnished bungalow on the edge of the bush behind Roseau. It hadn't been lived in for 6 months and we moved in at sundown one evening thinking we had the place to ourselves but soon realised we were not alone.

This was first evidenced by entering the toilet. As I opened the toilet door I noticed a missing vent in the window and as I went to close the door behind me I was confronted by a three-foot-long lizard who turned towards me and gave me a quizzical look.

I immediately backed out of the toilet and closed the door. Next to the toilet was a shower room and the intervening wall had a gap at the top. So, I grabbed a chair from the lounge and placed it against the wall of the shower room to peer over the top to see if the lizard was still there. I then got the fright of my life, as there was a three-foot iguana on the wall behind me. This was even more ugly and hornier than the lizard in front of me.

So again, I nervously backed out of the door, grabbed some towels and stuffed them under the doors. Not surprisingly, we ate out that evening and had a few rum punches in a trendy bar called Le Robe Creole in town. However, the reptiles weren't the only unwelcome guests.

For the first few days in the bungalow, we thought someone was lodging in the roof. As we walked through the bungalow, we would hear scuttling above us. Everywhere we went the person or creature seemed to follow us, especially at night. We began to think it was either Gollum from the Lord of the Rings or something out of a scary movie.

We then realised we had a roof full of bats. Shortly after sundown, they would line up and fly out from under the corrugated tin roof then fly back later. Surprisingly some would lose their bearings and fly through the open window into the lounge whereupon they would drop to the floor. I would then have to cover them with a towel and relaunch them off the balcony.

That was nothing compared to what would happen later after a hurricane.

Getting Started

To Work: From Meat to Fruit 'n Veg

On my first day of work, I reported to the Ministry of Agriculture and was due to see the Permanent Secretary. Instead, I was met by Major Johnson, a colourful outgoing charming and charismatic character (and budding entrepreneur) who had previously been in the army and was now the General Manager of the Agricultural Marketing Board who then informed me that I would be working at the Marketing Board. Little did I know that I had been hijacked as I found out later that I was supposed to be assigned to the Agricultural Planning Unit.

The Marketing Board acted as a buyer of last resort i.e., it would buy any agricultural produce that the private sector was not interested in. This wouldn't have been so bad if the Government didn't also set artificially high prices that were paid to farmers.

As such, the Marketing Board always operated at a loss. I was then given the seemingly impossible task of making it profitable. Given my economic qualifications, I recommended some options such as lowering but guaranteeing prices paid to farmers but this was not accepted.

Wake Up - Smell the Coffee!

Although I was not related to Houdini, by unknown magic, or more likely pure chance, I found out that the Marketing Board owned a small run-down coffee plant on the edge of town that used to roast coffee that was called Café Noir – a brand that exists today. The plant consisted of a mud walled building with a corrugated but incomplete tin roof and equipment consisting of drying tables, grinders and a roaster that had seen better days. It had clearly fallen into disuse and indeed previous Arabica and Robusta coffee growers were now only using coffee trees as hedgerows and field boundaries.

I did a feasibility study and with the Major's local knowledge and experience, we set and agreed a guaranteed buying price with the Ministry and set a lucrative sales price. Meanwhile I went about getting international advice and a team to strip clean, oil and repair the equipment as well as repair the roof, secure the building and operate the plant. On the first trial run some 3 months later, we burnt the coffee only to be told that this was how they used to roast it, as the locals liked the burnt taste.

The major also had a creative flair, and as such able to design and produce some fancy packaging. Within a few trial weeks we were in production and turning a small profit, and later again with the Major's contacts we sold to other islands in the Caribbean as well as subsidise the Marketing Board which also subsidised farmers as a buyer of last resort i.e., buying produce which could not be sold commercially.

In the coffee plant it wasn't all plain sailing, for example we found matching supply and production with demand proved difficult at first and later we found our coffee was being sold in shops we hadn't supplied. That said it was a great enjoyable learning experience.

Moving on

Agricultural Planning Unit

After six intensive months in the Marketing Board, I was then seconded to the Ministry of Agriculture, Agricultural Planning Unit to work with locals undertaking agro-industrial feasibility studies. The unit wasn't however in the Government building but set up in a large shack in the Botanical Gardens that had existed for nearly 200 years.

The planning of the gardens were started in1889 to encourage crop diversification and provide farmers with propagated seedlings. Its owner, William Davies, sold the 16 hectares of land, formerly a sugar plantation within Bath Estate, to the government in 1891.

Planting of the gardens began in 1890. Its first curator was Charles Murray of the Royal Botanic Garden Edinburgh. He was replaced by Henry F. Green, who planned and laid out the grounds. Joseph Jones then took over its management in 1892, and remained involved throughout his life; Jones would also become the first Superintendent of the Imperial Department of Agriculture for the West Indies in 1898.

Botanists from Kew Gardens in England supplied a variety of tropical species from around the world. Though its primary purpose remained economic and experimental, Jones introduced ornamental plants to make the grounds attractive.

By the 1930s, it became known as one of the finest botanical gardens in the West Indies but as you will read later; the gardens were severely damaged by Hurricane David in 1979, which destroyed many of its impressive old trees. That said many plants have since been restored.

For those of a "botanical bent", the gardens include the Bois Kwaib (Sabinea Carinalis), which is Dominica's national tree and flower, as well as many other tropical trees and palms. Noted specimens include the cannonball tree (Couroupita Guianensis), banyan (Ficus Benghalensis), century palm (Coripha Umbraculifera), and ylang ylang (Cananga Odorata).

The two endemic lizard species, the Dominican ground lizard and the Dominican anole, one of which I am sure frequented my toilet, are common on the grounds of the Botanical Gardens.

It is also frequently visited by a variety of wild birds, including three species of hummingbirds, Carib grackles, and the green heron, not to mention a lake full of mosquitoes that buzzed in and around my wooden hut!

The Botanical Gardens were established over 100 years with trees from around the world. A beautiful setting, which did make up for the accommodation and persistent harassment from the mosquitoes breeding in the lake below. Whilst we did burn mosquito coils to keep the mosquitoes away' I did actually get an infection and blood poisoning in my leg. I believe in later life whilst working out in the bush in Ghana rehabilitating gold mines it afforded me immunity from misquote bites whilst my team went down with dengue and malaria.

Well unlike the Marketing Board, the Agriculture Planning Unit was staffed by 4 to 5, what I would call up-n-coming communists and analysts, and had access to a small-dedicated four-wheel drive Suzuki jeep that would bounce from one pothole to the next whilst ramming your head against the roof.

This was a fun vehicle if you were less than 5 feet high, had full suspension and not every yard of road would have a pothole. If you didn't bump your head on the roof, you'd be jarring your knees on the steering wheel or dashboard.

It was useful for field trips as my Hillman Avenger, which I brought out from for the UK, took some serious bashing during its life in Dominica. So much so that the petrol tanks and exhausts pipe were ripped off going over potholes. As spares were difficult to obtain, I had to replace the fuel tank with a boat tank in the boot and attach the end of a vacuum cleaner pipe to the exhaust.

If that wasn't bad enough I was getting a ripped tyre fixed in a garage and the mechanics young son, who could not have been older than seven, got into the car and drove it backwards through the garage wall. That became a bit of a habit for some as you will find out later and finally I cannot believe I later brought the car back to the UK!

Anyway, back to the story. The Agricultural Planning Unit cum shack kept me busy undertaking market studies and financial and economic evaluations in an endeavour to support the diversification of the economy from its dependence on bananas.

I was always rushing around and hence earned the nicknamed "Rushford", as compared with some of the locals, even walking would seem like rushing to them.

Yet still, every assignment had its moments. These are outlined below confirming most people's views on the questionable value of economists.

The Adorable "Big Fluffy" White Rabbit Project

To improve the nutrition of Dominicans I was assigned the "Rabbit Project".

The objective was to breed Venezuelan great white rabbits and pilot breeding programs placing a buck and two does each with 6 farmers.

As the economist and renowned project manager (?) I evaluated the project in terms of the required breeding cycle, feed, cages and cash flow, thus requiring 11 cages to sell the rabbits after reaching 6 weeks of age.

It all seemed sensible and feasible. The Ministry persuaded six farming families spread around the island to participate and when the rabbits arrived, I got them checked out by the Vet who had a lab in the Botanical Gardens and placed them separately in their cages so that they could get used to them. After a couple of days, I then transported them carefully to the farms and instructed the farmers on feeding, exercise and breeding etc. and visited them every week to see how they were getting on.

All seemed to be going very well, the rabbits were breeding and the kitts, kitties or as everyone knows them, as "bunnies" were keeping healthy, growing and fattening up fast.

Around the 6th to 7th week when I visited to see how the "bunnies" were and how they would be sold on I was shocked. My project was ruined.

The project turned out to be a total failure as the farmer's wives and children refused to sell them and let them go, and instead kept the rabbits as pets!

What do the experts say – never work with animals especially big fluffy white ones?

The Limes Project

Limes might be small but this was a mammoth project. Traditionally L Rose and Co, a renowned British company, had established processing plant and estates on the island but over time a lack of investment and more competitive produce coming available from Latin America led to the gradual decline in sales and production. Furthermore, L Rose & Co adopted a caretaker approach to their plant replacing senior management with junior managers whilst selling off most of their estates. It seemed only a matter of time before they pulled out.

In undertaking my study, I conducted many field trips to assess the cost and profit from production and assess whether it would be feasible to invest in new tree stock and increased production.

The final business case was produced with the help of a senior economist from the British Development Office in Barbados and whilst it proved to be marginally in favour of reinvestment, the plug was pulled, and it was not taken forward.

I found out later the decision not to proceed had been taken by the British government before I even conducted the study.

The Notorious "Sniff the Farm" Book - Keeping Project

Now this seemed to be a promising project aimed at training farmers to keep simple records and accounts showing costs and profits from their farms. Moreover, as I was training to be a management accountant I was given the job.

On one such occasion, I travelled to meet a farmer who lived in Portsmouth in the north. I set off early from Roseau at 6 am and by 7am was passing through the outskirts of Portsmouth and heading up a mountain to the farm when I noticed a native Dominican leaning against a tree by the side of the road seemingly starring into thin air. I thought it strange for a local to be up so early and not moving. Usually this only happens when it is raining.

I then met with the farmer who had been nominated by the Ministry and we left the road and trekked up to the top of mountain where his small farmstead stood. This consisted of a couple of shacks, some chickens running around loose and a mistress who definitely was loose, but evidently did the cooking, cleaning and no doubt other chores!

In one shack was a kitchen and dining room, which we entered, whereupon we pulled out some old wooden chairs and sat down at his dining table. We then proceeded to map his farm on paper. His farm covered a few acres of what seemed to be mainly barren earth intersected with some patches of corn and sweet potato.

We then set out to walk the perimeter of his farm.

I was beginning to think that this was going to be a total waste of time and suggested we should take a short cut back to the shacks. I then stepped through a hedgerow to see an acre of very well-kept spiky plants – which seemed of dubious origin, but sure, I'd seen pictures of them on T-shirts or somewhere.

We then retired to one of his shacks and spent a couple of hours producing records and accounts and working out how much super profit he was making from his little "green" enterprise.

On completion, I was pleasantly surprised when he produced a bottle of Smuggler whisky from the cupboard, which I thought, was rather befitting the occasion. It also went down well with the freshly killed and cooked jerk chicken served up by his mistress. To top it all he also offered me some small hot bell peppers to eat with the chicken.

Wow! Hot? Mouth explodes like a fire from a dragon or furnace! That said, being British I tried to keep a straight face and stiff upper lip. Really was difficult. My lips and tongue were burning, eyes creased, went Chinese, weeping, with tears streaming from both eyes, streaming down my stricken face.

This went on for several minutes, and the burning sensation that concentrated in my mouth, throat and stomach was only slightly eased by the whisky, which I belched down to kill the pain followed by what seemed a gallon of water to quench the flames.

Meanwhile he laughed, and then I managed to laugh – that is, when I could eventually get my face straight and back into some working order.

After some coffee even more water, and a rest, the farmer then escorted me back to my jeep – a long walk that helped me sober up even under the mid-afternoon sun.

I then drove back down into Portsmouth and to my surprise spied the same guy I had seen in the morning still leaning against the tree! I had to stop to check if I was imagining it and was about to get out of the car to check if he was dead but he then winked and waved his hand at me.

I will always remember that moment for the rest of my life. Mebbe he was a ghost or an angel or mebbe a government spy. On the other hand, mebbe he was just chillin. Who knows?

The next day I visited the Ministry of Agriculture and the government official responsible for the farm project asked me if I had a good trip. I wasn't quite sure what he meant so I just nodded and smiled.

Somehow, I know he had already spoken to the farmer and nothing was ever mentioned about the trip – up until now.

The Catholic Church, Sister Mary and an Act of God

The Permanent Secretary asked if I would help Sister Mary who worked for the Catholic Church.

She wanted to finance a regional development program in the north east of the island and needed someone to do a feasibility study. The program was quite stretching and included tree felling and logging, community hospitals, farming and housing relocation.

I made many trips to the region to specify the requirements and develop business cases and an overall programme plan.

As Dominica is rich in high valued timber, including giant redwoods it was decided to launch a logging business first. This would the help finance the community hospitals and farming and housing schemes.

The case was made; outline plans, designs and bills of quantities were produced and presented.

Go ahead was given to the logging project, and the equipment was ordered, imported and crews employed, landed on the 28h August 1979, and ready to roll out.

The next day, would you believe it the trees fell down all on their own, many trees in the forest fell down on or close to roads ready to be hauled out. Hence, they did not need to be cut. It was truly an act of god even though the name associated with it was mine David, from Hurricane David.

Two weeks later having in some way supported this so-called act of god I woke one morning opened the door of my house to find a crate of whisky. Later that evening Sister Mary returned and much to the amusement of my dear wife managed to empty one of the twelve bottles.

"Many years later whilst completing another successful assignment involving a review of the Augusta Victoria Hospital in Jerusalem, a UN Funded hospital for Palestinian Refugees on a protected site atop the Mount of Olives, the senior Matron – a very big woman by all standards - shared a bottle of 7-star Metaxa with me. To this day I still can't remember how I got to bed that night but that assignment was another story which may one day be revealed".

The Blood Bank - My Wife's Project

As for my dear wife, who had previously worked for Barclays Bank, including working in the Head Office in Canon St, London in the UK, she found she could not get a job in a bank in Dominica even working for free, as it would (in their words) create the wrong impression. I wonder if such reverse discrimination would be allowed today.

My wife however did work part time for a charity aided blood bank and again had to deal with prejudice, such as excuses and resistance to giving blood on the basis that the persons involved would feel the blood drain from their body, and would not be able to use their limbs, or worse still that their sex life would be seriously impaired.

Such was the resistance that many expats including myself were giving blood more or less every 6 weeks and sometimes in an emergency on a Saturday morning after a heavy night out on the town the night before.

Still, she persevered, overcame the prejudices, and thanks to her and other people's efforts there has been a thriving blood bank clinic in Dominica to this very day.

Life on a Caribbean Island

So much for the work, so what was life like on the island, which is aptly named as the "Nature Island of the Caribbean" ?

Having seen "Lost" the American TV series and having read "Robinson Cruse" I sometimes draw vivid comparisons, though clearly there weren't so many life and death experiences to be faced, or were there?

In addition, working and living in a virtual paradise island does have its advantages and disadvantages. I always remember imagining a golden halo sitting over the UK combined with the smell of sausages, pork pies and salt 'n vinegar crisps wafting in the air, all of which you could not get in Dominica.

In many cases though, it was though like paradise – rich in fauna, volcanic mountains and lakes, hot water springs, long unspoiled sandy beaches and cheap booze.

On a different matter whilst I was kept busy at work, rushing around, and living up to my nickname, my wife apart from a sprint doing charity work in the Blood Bank, spent much of her time in the house, and apart from occasional visits, clearly missed her family and friends.

That said life is what you make it...

Culinary Pleasure

With regards generally to food obviously bananas were plentiful, but there were also many varieties of fruit and vegetables. It took a while to get used to dasheen and sweet potato and it was not possible to get English potatoes, like King Edwards.

A particularly tasty dish of bananas involved putting green (unripe bananas) into a stew locally called a "jot" to which fish would typically be added.

Fruit in general was large, juicy, varied, and plentiful. Mangoes were particularly large and juicy and strange fruits such as Dorian which I mentioned were grown too.

However, for me the most delicious and most refreshing fruit was the "jelly" coconut, which is immature and containing internal soft white flesh and full of milk. Moreover, in my view there is nothing better than walking up a mountain in the morning and drinking the cool juice from a coconut, which has just bee freshly cut from the tree.

Moreover, of course, you will not be far from spices in the Caribbean. Indeed, across from our house was an abandoned plantation, which used to grow nutmegs and other spices and was then used to pasture cattle. I used to gather the spices and have to admit I also used to collect the cattle dung and grow tomatoes and fruits in the back garden.

To avoid insects, I grew the tomatoes in boxes outside under the kitchen window fed from water outflowing from the sink. To my surprise one day, I went into the kitchen to find a load of baby frogs that emerged from the boxes and were jumping all over the kitchen.

Of course, the biggest jumper besides me repeatedly hitting what I thought was a live (but actually dead) 12-inch poisonous centipede[1] on the kitchen floor with a cooking pan one morning whilst worrying about my private parts and jumping around in the nude, is indeed the Mountain Chicken - the delicacy of Dominica. It is indeed a mountain bullfrog, aptly named because of its size, whereabouts and taste, that of Kentucky Fried Chicken when cooked. Besides Vegans it would no doubt put some people off.

Locally chicken and goat were always available. In the supermarkets, you could always get the best cuts, as the locals preferred the back, feet and necks.

As for eating goat, the locals would often boil a whole goat in an oil drum and make a stew. This was popular especially in Juve or carnival and was used to line the stomach in advance of numerous quantities of rum.

You could also get English beef, which had evidently been rejected by the USA. Ironically, we would trade this with expats and crew that cruised with the Geest banana boats that plied from the Caribbean to the UK. These boats would dock in Roseau and then proceed to Portsmouth in the north of the island before returning to Cardiff. Often we would stay on board and enjoy the good food and parties held for the twelve paying guests. On one night, they had to throw me off at Portsmouth as I was enjoying myself so much I tried to hide out as a stowaway. More later.

Finally, of course there was the fast-food joints. My favourite was the Le Robe Creole. They had great hamburgers with salad and a friendly bar. One night I was at the bar with Gordon Bosson a Development Officer from the British Overseas Development Agency in Barbados. A local farmer kept listening in and butting into our conversation so we invented the "sheep project".

We explained to the farmer that the Welsh had bred sheep with their right legs longer than their left so they could more easily walk round hills and hence could eat more grass and put on more weight in a shorter period, and we mentioned we were looking for farmers to conduct trials. We also said that we would throw in a sheep dog as well. Well, the farmer took it hook line and sinker and wanted to sign up there and then.

Rum Shop Dogs

As we were living on the edge of the bush, we decided to get some guard dogs.

Just down the road from us was a rum shop. Well actually like many places dotted around the island they served as what we would call in England corner shops, which were convenience stores or little community/ village-based retail outlets where one could purchase basic foodstuffs and everyday household items. We purchased a large Alsatian Labrador called "Bruce" who was loving and friendly then took pity on his adopted little buddy "Buster" who was 10 times more trouble than his size and who turned out to be the leader of the gang.

Most people kept dogs to guard their houses most of which did not have fences so the dogs would roam where they liked with borders or territories determined by the dogs themselves and where they cocked their leg. Occasionally these borders would be disputed and on one occasion two fierce Alsatians from a nearby house charged and attacked Bruce and had him quickly pinned to the ground on our front lawn. Hearing this little Buster raced down form the upstairs balcony of the house and attacked one of the Alsatian dogs ...biting his leg and holding onto it. Both Alsatians ran off with Buster still holding onto the leg of one of them.

Buster was always the tough adventurous type, always getting into mischief and causing trouble. Once we went to the airport to pick up my wife's parents who had come to visit us. We took the dogs and left them in the carpark aside the airport, with the windows open, enough for them to breathe.

Whilst waiting in the Arrivals Hall we heard a commotion outside. Looking out we saw several airport officials running across the runway chasing a small black dog. We then realized it was Buster, our dog. We owned up to the officials that Buster was our dog and I was then instructed by the officials to go onto the runway to retrieve him whilst an incoming flight was put on a holding pattern. The in-laws who were on the flight then duly arrived albeit a little late and we ferried them through the customs to the car.

We thought that would be the end of it. Except on the way back to Roseau Buster was sick, and spat out a lizard's tail which continued to wiggle on the back seat between the in-laws...... they were not impressed. Welcome to Dominica!

Whilst Buster was a strong little dog, he was also a bit tubby. Every morning he would tour the local houses ending up at the top of our street in a friend's household seeking breakfast. Pete the owner was a teacher at the Technical College just outside Roseau. One morning Pete, albeit a little late, was setting off to the College and was driving down the road with the window open when Buster saw him and jumped through the open window then in excitement urinated all over his tropical suit. The language heard was definitely blue and Scottish as Pete returned home to get changed.

Perhaps, it was the food we fed the dogs, plus the odd lizard they captured themselves. As you could not get tinned dog food we kept a pot of rice on the go into which vegetable peelings, cheap meat and fish would be added. Surprisingly the dogs could fillet the bones out of the fish themselves.

Rotary Club

In terms of charitable work, I also joined the Rotary Club of Dominica, which was very active in both charity work and organising social events.

Coming from the UK, Rotary in Dominica was more like Roundtable, where I used to be an active member of the Ruislip Branch in West London, who did a lot of community work. Many fond memories remain. For example, we used to run a Xmas float with Santa and give toys to children in their houses in the evening, in return for any small contribution, which we would then give to local charities.

Whilst advertised in advance (and mebbe that caused the following - who knows) Santa would disappear sometimes for an hour or so. Well, the so-called "tropic of Ruislip" as it was then known did have a reputation for after hour's activities of a hot steamy kind. As a backup, we kept a spare Santa costume just in case.

The Xmas event was our major fund raiser in the year but we also ran many other successful events such as a fun-fair at the Lido (a local water and bathing resort), car boot sales, auctions, music gigs and other social events, raising money for local schools, hospitals and welfare activities.

Surprising for some, the priority project, which we funded in Dominica through cricket matches, beach parties and dances, was the setting up of a mental hospital; interestingly mental illness was allegedly deemed the biggest illness on the island due to inbreeding over many centuries.

In Rotary, we thus attended many dances and parties, which were great fun. Sometimes the dancing would get out of hand with partners almost joined and rotating at the hip, shuffling their feet and wiggling their bums to the beat. It was sometimes difficult not to have an embarrassing moment where more than just the temperature would rise.

Friends

Through Rotary, it was easy to make friends. In particular, we made friends with an American couple, Carol and Alan Bunting who had built a large wooden lodge in a deep valley far up the Layou River. From their veranda or pool, you could look down the valley and watch the sun go down. When it was raining, you would often spot triple rainbows and after a few drinks supposedly see the green lantern – a green flash above the sea – just as the sun disappears behind the watery horizon. Personally, I reckoned it was the colour of the lime reflected in the glasses of gin and tonic!

Seriously, though, Alan was a Vietnam vet who had been hit by a dum-dum bullet and given his lasts rights before surviving and being decommissioned from the US marines. He ran a motorbike rental shop in Roseau whilst his wife Carol ran the house and six dogs.

One such dog resembled Scooby Doo – a big bundling Great Dane - for whom she would hold birthday parties and lavish all the pooches with huge chocolate cakes whilst we feasted on pork, beans, and a case of beer.

Often, we would stay there until the early hours and see the sunrise. On the night of our wedding anniversary, after a few too many drinks, and typically ignoring my advice, my wife insisted she would drive home.

Well… she reversed the car in a straight line without looking back up the long snaking drive and as such slammed the car into a giant redwood. All I could do was roll out of the car and lie on the drive to be picked up by Alan, both of us splitting our sides laughing.

The Car: Hilman Avenger

I am surprised the Hilman Avenger lasted the two years in Dominica as we often ventured inland to explore the many beautiful rivers and lakes or would track up the coast to enjoy beaches at the weekend or simply go shopping in town, and even go to the cinema when it was on. I say on, often the film in the cinema would break down, but if so, you were given a ticket to come again. We didn't mind even though most of the films were Kung Fu.

The House

Our house was located west of Roseau on the edge of the bush and comprised a first floor with three small bedrooms, one en-suite, a lounge, kitchen and balcony. There was also a small flat below which was used by the landlord when visiting from Barbados, and it was adjoined to an open garage space, with a small garden front and rear of the house.

Being on the edge of the bush and a ridge than ran into a forested hill, security was an issue, and everyone in the neighbourhood had guard dogs.

We purchased two dogs from a rum shop, which was the term we used for a wooden shack with one side containing a bar and the other, a small grocery store, accessed through a swing door.

This always reminded me of Westerns, the films where the gunslingers in the Wild West rode into town, slung the reigns of their horse on a rail, stepped up and threw open the swing doors of the Saloon. With both hands on their gun holsters, and face hidden under a dusty cowboy hat, they would stroll to the bar and order a shot, and as the barman reaches down under the bar for a shot gun the cowboy cocks a gun against his head and says "Mister, just give me the bottle and not the gun, or I will have your head before you can run!"

Yep The Wild West runs in the veins.

Daylight Robbery

Anyway, the dogs, for the most part, did their duty and barked at anyone who approached the house. It remained secure except on one occasion we were invited up the valley to our friends

Pete n Pam and upon invitation took the dogs with us. When we returned our dogs started barking and ran round the back of the house.

I gave chase but by the time I got round the back the intruders were long gone. We entered the house to find that the kitchen had been broken into through forced security bars on a window, with food stolen from the freezer along with some kitchen knives. Fortunately, they could not get access to the rest of the house as we had locked the intervening door.

We reported it to the police and a few days later, they informed us that they had found some knives while searching a house and asked us to identify and confirm that they were ours. We did so and was then asked to attend court to testify against two local teenagers. To our surprise, the teenagers were not charged, as we had not specified the value of the goods that were stolen. We were, of course, never asked what the value was, but let it go.

The Gardener, the Maid, and the Local Bobby

Honest -, it wasn't that the wife was lazy, indeed she struggled to find things to do, but all expats were expected to recruit gardeners and maids and we were no exception.

The gardener helped me terrace the hill behind the house and grow vegetables and I even managed to grow tomatoes in a wooden box under the outflow pipe from the kitchen sink. However, this proved to be a favourite nesting spot for frogs and on occasion, we would get a load of baby frogs hopping across the kitchen sink. This was quite comical though we were on the edge of the bush and one had to be wary of creatures that are more dangerous.

The most dangerous creature was the centipede, which has scales and is scary. They can grow up to a foot long, scuttle, and weave across the floor like a snake. They have two nasty fang-like horns on their head and if not careful rise up, bite and inject you with poison that inflicts serious pain and swelling. Most people are actually bitten whilst asleep in their bed, which is probably even scarier. To protect ourselves we put insecticide on the floors.

One morning I was walking bare foot and indeed bare below the waist and stepped gingerly into the kitchen to see a large centipede on the floor. Without hesitation, I grabbed a large iron pan from the sink and hit it with force. To my surprise it bounced up off the floor so when it landed

I hit it again, and again to my surprise it bounced even higher. I was about to hit it again when I noticed it was not moving. I then realised it had been dead all the time. Well, you just cannot be too careful!

The maid was a young local girl that we hired to clean and do the ironing. She was a sweet little thing though did cause us some problems besides the usual lapses of attendance explained by every excuse under the sun. The most notable was her lapse of memory such as leaving the iron on the ironing board whilst it burnt all the way through or tying Buster the dog to the leg of a four-poster bed which he managed to chew through while she cleaned the house.

The only other regular visitor was the local Bobby (policeman) who was an industrious young man who approached me one day whilst I was mauling the grass on the front lawn with a blunt machete. He asked if he could graze his cow on it. I thought this was a great idea. I wasn't expecting anything else except that one day the cow was gone and the next the Bobby turned up at the door with the hind quarter of the cow over his shoulder, which he presented to me with a smile.

Ever slaughtered the hindquarter of a cow with a blunt machete? All I can say is that the whole kitchen was covered in meat, bone, blood and blubber, which we eventually managed to bag and put into a chest freezer. The meat lasted for months.

The Neighbours

Down the lane where we lived and opposite were the Astafans, a wealthy family with a mansion and the two Alsatians I mentioned before, that used to run wild. The Astafans also ran a chain of supermarkets by that name but largely kept themselves to themselves.

Opposite them were the Carbons, Tom Carbon the elder was a wryly character, retired, full of wit and charm, who liked the odd gin on consecutive days. He would visit occasionally and we would have a laugh whilst the women were banned to the kitchen - as was the custom of the island in those days!

On one occasion, he brought with him his brother who looked much like him, though Tom at one point in the evening mentioned that his brother was much darker than him,. inferring he was of inferior status. I took it lightly.

Tom also had a very pretty articulate and outgoing daughter that worked in the local radio station every morning brightening up everyone's day.

Places to Go

Well, I highlight in this chapter many of the wonderful places to go. There are many more than I can describe but a thorough tour of the coast and inland is definitely a must. When I look back many years later, I still get a tingle down my spine, and the fact I can remember so much so vividly all the places my wife and I visited, and what happened in the two years we were there, is a testament to how great the island truly is.

I set out some of the places to go. My wife and I didn't go to all of the places you can now see in a Tourist guide and in one sense if you visit you should make your own plans which will undoubtedly change as you journey through this beautiful island beckons. I set out some guidance on the places we visited and experienced, and when I look back I still wonder at the sheer beauty of the island and the overall friendliness of the people.

Carib Reserve

Well, let me start with a historical yet strange "must see" which I still can't quite comprehend and understand. For those not interested in the history skip the next few pages and go to "Our Visit....."

The indigenous Caribs (Kalinago), who number about 3000 people, are a minority in Dominica. They are unique in being the last community in the Caribbean that claims direct descent from the indigenous Kalinago who originally populated the entire region before the arrival of European colonizers. The Kalinago themselves were exterminated or driven from neighbouring islands.,

Going back in time the Amerindian people settled the Caribbean island chain as far back as c3100bc The hunter-gatherer Ortoiroid people settled Dominica from about 3000bc to 400bc, to the modern day Kalinago who date back to about 1000AD.

These earlier people came from South America, having travelled down the Orinoco and up the island chain bringing with them their staple foods: corn and cassava

Known to the Kalinago as Wai'tukubli, Dominica's rugged terrain worked to their advantage as they held back European settlers for centuries.

Agreed to remain a neutral territory, Dominica was the last Caribbean island to be colonized by Europeans. Instead, Dominica served as a stopping off point for refuelling ships and refreshing crews after their long transatlantic voyage.

In the time of sailing vessels, the passage between Dominica and Guadeloupe became the main route for ships traveling from Europe. This was due to the ocean currents and northeast trade winds, which created a natural course for ships sailing west. At this time, the Kalinago traded with Europeans while still protecting their land.

The Kalinago appoint and have their own chief. They tend to keep to themselves and their culture has remained very much unchanged compared to other areas of the island.

They reputedly use 300 different herbs for medicine — some of the best bush doctors hail from the Territory. Dances, traditions, legends, and beliefs have been kept alive by the elders who pass on these traditions through story-telling.

The language is only spoken by a few people today and traditional dances are performed by Karifuna, their dance group.

The Kalinago Territory is well worth a visit. It is almost spiritual how one is flung centuries back into a cool, calm place with the most beautiful group of people, amidst the straw huts and baskets made by the best artisans. You might never want to leave but you would have to unless you could prove that you have Kalinago ancestry!

The Kalinago on Dominica fought against the Spanish and later European settlers for two centuries. Over time, however, their population declined and they were forced into remote regions of the island as European settlers and imported African slaves grew in number on the island.

The first reservation of land for the Kalinago people occurred in 1763, when 232 acres (0.94 km2) of mountainous land and rocky shoreline around Salybia, on the east coast, were set aside by British colonial authorities as part of the surveying of the island and its division into lots.

A legend arose that this land was set aside by the request of Queen Charlotte, the wife of George III; from this another legend spread, and persisted among some Kalinago to the present, that Charlotte had set aside half of Dominica for the Kalinago people.

Later colonial officials were unable to locate any record of a title deed for the 232 acres (0.94 km2), however. European settlers continued attempts to turn the Kalinago lands into plantations through the end of the 18th century, but the Kalinago successfully held out, often with the assistance of runaway slaves.

In 1902, Henry Bell, the Administrator of Dominica, sent a lengthy report to the Colonial Office on the state of the Kalinago people after he had visited its communities. He proposed that 3,700 acres (roughly 2% of Dominica's area) be set aside for the Kalinago, and that a Kalinago "chief" be officially recognized and given a token annual allowance of 6 pounds.

Bell's proposals were adopted in 1903, formally establishing the "Carib Reserve". Its boundaries were announced in the Official Gazette of Dominica on 4 July 1903. . It is made up of eight villages – Sineku, Mahaut River, Gaulette River, Salybia, Crayfish River, Bataka, Atkinson and part of Concord.

The Kalinago Chief was subsequently endowed with a silver-headed staff, and a ceremonial sash embroidered with "The Chief of the Caribs" in gothic lettering.

At the time the "Carib Reserve" was established, the Kalinago population of around 400 was extremely isolated from the rest of Dominica, but the community appreciated the token symbols.

"The Carib War"

The population of the "Carib Reserve" remained disconnected from the rest of Dominica, seldom seen and largely self-sustaining, apart from some limited illegal trade with the neighbouring French islands of Marie Galante and Martinique.

The colonial Administrator decided to crack down on this smuggling due to its impact on revenues, and in 1930, five armed policemen entered the Territory to seize smuggled goods and to arrest suspects. When the police tried to seize a quantity of rum and tobacco and to take away suspects in Salybia, a crowd gathered in response and hurled stones and bottles.

The police fired into the crowd, injuring four, of whom two later died. The police were beaten but managed to escape to Marigot, without having seized prisoners or contraband.

The Administrator responded by summoning the Royal Navy light cruiser HMS *Delhi* to the coast, which fired star shells into the air and displayed searchlights along the shore; the Kalinago ran in fear from this display of force and hid in the woods.

Finally, Marines landed to aid local police in the search for the perpetrators of the disturbance.

Accurate news of the incident was difficult to come by, and rumours instead spread throughout the island of a Kalinago uprising. *The Times* incorrectly reported that Kalinago had looted and rioted in the capital, Roseau. The incident is still hyperbolically known as "The Carib War."

Kalinago Chief Jolly John subsequently surrendered to authorities in Roseau and was charged, with five other Kalinago, with wounding the police officers and theft, though the prosecution fell apart by the following year.

A commission of inquiry was appointed in 1931 by the Governor of the Leeward Islands to investigate the 1930 incident and the situation of the Kalinago generally. The final report found fault on all sides.

Consequently, for the Kalinago, the position of Chief was eliminated, the staff and sash were confiscated, and the former chief was forbidden to call himself "king.

Our Visit to the Carib Reserve

We visited the reserve on a sunny afternoon and were amazed by sight of so many friendly faces going about their daily chores of cooking and cleaning. The villages seemed very neat and tidy, full of vibrant colour, reflected in flowing dresses, green grass skirts, beads and headbands.

What was truly amazing was the shape of some of the women's eyes – to me very Chinese but definitely from Latin America - and the deep oily brown colour of their skins, looking so different from other Dominicans.

In addition, there were many shops and frontages of wooden shacks adorned with a colourful array of baskets, weaved ornaments, clothing, pottery and beads, which were sold to clearly supplement their income.

Dominica Museum

The Dominica Museum is the national museum of Dominica, located in the capital, Roseau, on a quay in front of the Old Market of Roseau, where I used to work. During colonial times, it was the centre for slave trading and was formerly an old market building and a post office dating to 1810.

Dominica's most notable historian, Lennox Honychurch, has been responsible for much of the museum. The Dominica Museum contains general items related to the cultural and social history and geology and archeology of Dominica.

These include old photographs, photographs and portraits of past rulers, colonial furniture, including a chair and old cabinet and a barometer, specimens of birds and fishes, colonial agricultural items and indigenous cultural articles including the Pwi Pwi, a miniature form of raft, a replica of a Carib hut and Arawak pottery and tools.

Of note are some stone axes, some of them reaching nine inches in length. The museum also contains displays related to the Volcanology of the island, and artifacts related to the early settlers also include oars, domestic implements, wooden figurines and old musical instruments. Truly worth the visit

Fort Young

Situated near Roseau Cathedral, on the quay, the hotel which has about 70 rooms was established in 1964 and sits within the ramparts of the old colonial military Fort Young which was established in the 1770s.

After we landed we stayed at the hotel for about six weeks. It was strange in one sense in that everything was different. The typical culture shock when venturing into a completely different land, environment and culture never mind that we were two of less than 100 white people amongst 7000 black people on the island at that time.

On the other hand, it was like a second honeymoon. The hotel had by no surprise an old historical look and feel about it – a sort of Victorian colonial atmosphere created through refurbishment amidst ancient battlements overlooking the sea.

The rooms were spacious, well decorated in different bright fabrics and colours and the bathrooms contained large old sunken baths.Of course I would remember that piece of information. Also the restaurant on the seafront was well laid out and the swimming pool was set in what I think must have been the parade ground. Every Friday there would be a band playing and the bar served some really exotic (way -out) cocktails.

Yep definitely another Honeymoon setting.

La Robe Creole

At the time and probably still is, one of the best restaurants in the capital, La Robe Creole sits on the second floor of a colonial house, beside a sunny plaza on a slope above the sea.

Well, you could not but visit a simple wooden café bar that serves great burgers and drinks and has a convivial warm and friendly atmosphere. No wonder it is still there and I believe it has expanded downstairs with a take-away and much more!

Even then, the staff, dressed in madras Creole costumes, serve food in a long, narrow dining room capped with heavy beams and filled with 19th-century relics. You could enjoy pumpkin-pimento soup, Callaloo with cream of coconut soup, crab backs (when in season), and shrimp in coconut with garlic sauce. For dessert, was banana or coconut cake or ice cream. Or if like me just hit the bar and have a beer and a chat with the locals!

Now I believe, at street-level, is a section of the restaurant called The Mouse Hole (open Mon-Sat 7:30am-4pm), which is a good place for food on-the-go. You can buy freshly made sandwiches, salads, and light meals. They also still make good Trinidad-inspired rotis.

On one occasion when frequenting the old bar with a colleague from the Overseas Development Agency in Barbados one local guy who had drunk a few too many rums kept interrupting us and asking what we did as a job. So, we concocted the following story about the short-legged mountain goat.....

We stated we were on a secret project to breed mountain goats with two right legs shorter than the left so that goats could walk clockwise around mountains and not fall over. He tried it and immediately fell over. We then informed him that it only works on goats. He then became somewhat confused and thankfully left. Don't worry he's probably not there anymore.

Papillote- Tropical Nature Resort

On several occasions we went to Papillote a restaurant up the Layou valley close to a series of waterfalls. The restaurant is famous for having a jacuzzi cut out of a rock and fed by a hot water spring. It is also famous for being in a tropical rain forest set against mountains and waterfalls and full of wildlife including of course butterflies from whence the name derives. Finally, as for the restaurant there is no better way to have deserts coffees and liquors after a meal, than sat in the jacuzzi.

Caution: It was then however a remote isolated location and indeed not a place to leave your car overnight as you may not see most of it come the morning.

This almost happened to us as on one afternoon we went to the falls with our dogs one beingthe small puppy named Buster, the bull dog/ terrier we purchased from a rum shop. The other Bruce, a Labrador / Collie. Unfortunately, when we got to the top of the falls Buster fell in and was being dragged by the current toward the brim of the falls, with inevitable consequences.

Seeing this sudden turn of events, without thinking I then instinctively dived in fully clothed to rescue him whereupon sensing the falls looming up ahead, Buster frantically turned and managed to paddle to the river edge. I then stopped, was able to stand and took off my jeans and t-shirt in the water and put them on the riverbank to dry. Well, that was the end of the expedition to the falls, or was it?

Later after my clothes had dried off a bit we decided to return to the car. Reaching for the keys in my jean pocket, I realized my keys must have fallen out somewhere, and then it dawned on me it must have been in the falls.

Panic set in. Thoughts of returning next morning to find the car with no wheels kept flashing in my mind. Slowly we returned to the falls with eyes peeled to the ground and eventually reached the falls but could see nothing in the swirling water.

By the time, we got back to the car it was starting to get dark. Then out of the bushes a little local boy not more than six or seven years old appeared and asked us what the problem was. I explained and he said he would find the keys.

Reluctantly and with a lot of pessimism - but with little other options available - I returned with him to the falls. He dived in and was under water for what seemed like an eternity then returned after a few minutes with the keys in his hand. I could not believe it. In addition, I was a qualified sub aqua diver. Needless to say, he was amply rewarded and, with deeply found gratitude, we were able to drive home.

The Boiling Lake

Again, I am surprised the car lasted the two years in Dominica, as mentioned we often ventured inland to explore the many beautiful rivers and lakes most notable of which was the second largest boiling lake in the world. This is reached by trekking several hours through jungle, mountain and rivers, and ultimately stepping through sulphuric pools in the Valley of Desolation.

Unfortunately, when you get there you may find, as we did, that you cannot see the lake because of the mist and fumes. Still well worth the hike and on the return journey you can enjoy the hot springs and waterfalls, also the way back seemed quicker, partly of course, as its downhill much of the way.

When we did this trek, there was a path but steps were very high. I think you need to be reasonably fit to do this walk as it's quite arduous, and it can get hot and sticky, as well as slippery, given the mud, wet rocks and streams that need to be traversed.

In addition, we went with a guide although these days I guess you could use GPS. We also set off early at 7am and got back late afternoon. Yes quite a long hike, but that said, it is a trip of a lifetime!

So, as for the trail, firstly, the departure to the Boiling Lake starts at Titou Gorge, which can be reached by car.

The first part of the journey involves hiking up a path through the forest. It's a steep climb which is awarded after an hour or so by dropping down to a small river where we had a short breakfast and break.

We then proceeded up to Mount Nicholl, another climb or should I say steep walk, again to be rewarded, this time with a view of the coast, villages and towns, including Roseau. We then dropped down into the Valley of Desolation witnessing an incredible change in scenery from lush green vegetation to barren red, orange, yellow and whitened rock, interspersed with strong smelling sulphur and boiling water pools.

You could have been in a sci-fi movie on an alien planet made even more real by the sharp strong smell of sulphur. In addition, we had to tread carefully to avoid slipping or being scolded with the short intermittent spray from the hot pools.

Finally, we ascended a long hill to the Boiling Lake. A great sight even though, when we were there, much was covered in mist. However, it felt like a great achievement. Also, whilst I have been to many places on the planet, described as the "End" or "Edge of The World", this certainly ranked as one of them.

Because of the mist, we stayed on the brim of the volcanic crater and didn't venture down. We rested a short while, had a small lunch of sandwiches and did not stay long in view of the mist and the barren landscape. We also wanted to ensure we would get back before dark.

Therefore, we set off again and the way back seemed a lot easier. When we got closer to base, we stopped by a hot water spring and small waterfall. I could not resist it. I was truly in my element. As I write this, I think you'd definitely pay a lot of money elsewhere for this sort of treatment.

It also helped to clean all the sulphur off my skin and I felt truly refreshed. The others meanwhile washed by the side of the pool and rehydrated. It was then I wished I had an iced cold beer.

Anyway, it was not long before we got back to the car and were weaving our way back to Roseau, back home for another shower.... and, of course, a couple of well-earned beers.

Insert Image 8,

Emerald Pool, Trafalgar Pools and other pools
in Morne Trois, Pitons National Park

Emerald pool, located some 20 minutes from Roseau, is truly one of my favourite places to visit, unlike anything I had ever seen before. A beautiful spot in the island - essentially a shallow pool fed by a small waterfall surrounded by palm trees and bushes. What was so beautiful and intriguing is the colour of the water from which the pool gets its name.

*"This small lake set against a shear sided mountain glitters like an
emerald stone because of the minerals contained in the water".*

When one conjures up an image of green water one thinks of weed, slime or some chemical pollutant - but this is quite the opposite. Truly, like an emerald it sparkles in the light and is translucent. It almost has a magical, Disney film, feel and look about it, and well worth seeing and spending some time there just taking it all in.

I believe it now has a nature trail and has been in many movies.

Trafalgar Falls, also located in Morne Trois, Pitons National Park, is a UNESCO World Heritage site, again within easy reach by car from Roseau. It comprises twin falls – one named Daddy (75ft), and one named Mommy (125 ft) which flow in parallel.

When we were there, one could take a rough path to the falls and swim in a hot spring below. Now when you arrive you will see a visitor reception area built on a well-maintained path. Even from the reception, area there is a viewing platform. The waterfalls descend into small pools, which are easy to enter, and safe to swim but I believe the hot springs were destroyed by a landfall in 1995.

Mommy is the easier of the two falls to reach. However, slippery boulders which you have to navigate around can complicate the hike. The views though are spectacular.

The once taller waterfall, i.e. the one to the left, is also popularly referred to as the "Papa Falls" and the shorter, but stronger one is also affectionately called the "Mama Falls"; both on tributaries of the Roseau River. The "Breakfast" River that hikers cross en route to the Boiling Lake is one of those tributaries, and it tumbles into the shorter waterfall. The water that leaves the Freshwater Lake area flows through Ti-Tou Gorge before cascading in the Papa Falls.

Not visited but well worth the hike the falls at Tatou Gorge Middleham, and Jacko in Morne Trois are said to beautiful and swimmable. Victoria Falls, to the southeast, is also spectacular, and wilder and fast running.

Titou Gorge which is only about 10 minutes' drive from Roseau is also worth a visit and is now used for cannoning and jumping into water (rappelling), letting the water take you down river and over small waterfalls and rapids.

The Gorge has many waterfalls—nearly too many for us to name. Whether you're rappelling or taking a break to soak it all in, this is truly a magical place to be.

Layou River

Another favourite spot of ours was Layou River, which is up the coast from Roseau and is the largest river in Dominica. Easy to get to by road and ideal for a day trip. It's also relatively safe for families as even rapids are very shallow and mild.

The river is broad and again being very shallow, is full of small round boulders and pebbles and great for paddling in or rolling down river in the gentle current. Also the banks are large, flat, and firm to the feet, and ideal for pitching a tent, or laying out blankets for a picnic or BBQ.

Castaways - Coconut Beach

We would also go to BBQs on the Layou River or go up to Coconut Beach and enjoy the water sports. The water sports were not maintained and supervised, as they should have been then as on one occasion a fellow ex pat and I were out on a sailing dingy when the boom and the rudder broke, and we were swept by the current, taken out to sea and drifted down the coast. We drifted north past cliffs and bays and even further out to sea. Our options seemed limited as my friend could not swim and I was a lousy sailor.

It was a tough choice but my friend volunteered to enter the water and hold the rudder whilst I slowly tacked and sailed the boat back whilst keeping an eye out for sharks. We made slow progress and after several hours of darkness, we hailed a boat and managed to return to shore, cold, shivering wet, but happy.

"The drinks were supposedly on us that night, in fact the drinks ended up being on me!

Indian River

Indian River, near Portsmouth is worth a trip especially by canoe as in parts it's like paddling on a narrow river through a jungle and is quite wild but safe. I believe they now organize boat trips along it.

Cabrits

Also near Portsmouth is Cabrits, which in 1986 became a national park comprising forests, wetlands as well as coral reefs, which are good for diving. When we were there, it was famous for Fort Shirley, which overlooks the bay in Portsmouth, and it was alleged that within its ramparts it was inhabited by jumping spiders not that we saw any when we visited. It now also sports a Kempinski resort and hotel.

Scots Head

At the opposite end of the island, in the south, is Scotts Head, a fishing village overlooking Soufriere Bay, which is also good for diving as well as stunning views. It was named after Colonel George Scot who served in the British force that captured the island from the French in 1761. It also boasted a fort most of which has fallen into the sea. However the fort and the island was later recaptured by the French in 1778 before returning to the British in 1783 along with an exchange of other Caribbean islands, as a concession in the Treaty of Versailles.

Scuba Diving

Whilst there are so many beautiful places to visit and explore, perhaps too many to mention, for me the greatest places to visit were under the sea. As Dominica is a volcanic island, in many places the sea shelves drop off very quickly and are very steep giving rise to a wide variety of fish and underwater landscapes. I was fortunate enough to buddy up with Mike Pryn, a former British Navy diver, to lay lobster pots to catch crabs as well as enjoy spear fishing, off his small boat every weekend.

And of course, we had some interesting experiences and encounters.

Well, to start with, whilst Mike was a very good diver, he also liked playing pranks and tricks.

On one occasion, whilst connected to the boat by rope as we dived, we swam round a headland and I was spun round by the current, which then twisted the rope around me such that I could not move. Mike decided to leave me there helpless for 20 minutes whilst he went off spearfishing.

On another occasion we went into a wreck and he exited via a porthole whilst I swam into a barracuda.

On a more serious occasion, we were down about 80 feet when he signalled to me to wait whilst he dove deeper. After about 10 minutes and even less minutes of air I got a bit worried so dove a little deeper to see him spinning below with some large object. He looked in trouble so I descended to over 100 feet to see him spiralling almost out of control with a large turtle. When I got closer I realised he had illegally speared a turtle but was struggling with it. He then passed me the spear gun and signalled for me to do an emergency assent.

When we hit the surface, he asked for my tank of air and said he was diving again to decompress and that I should put the turtle in the boat, pick up a spare tank and do the same. This I did and descended quickly to about 30 feet and could not see him. I waited a few minutes then dived back down to 100 feet thinking he may be in trouble. After waiting a while, I then ascended slowly decompressing every 30 feet.

When I hit the surface, there he was sitting in the boat. He had descended 30 feet then swam off in a tangent. As I scrambled into the boat, he then warned me to be careful where I tread, as it was a snapping turtle. Classic!

A few weeks later, purely by accident, I got my revenge. We had lifted some pots and was heading back to shore so I decided to go spear fishing. He told me we were over a spot where he knew two parrotfish that would always guide him to bigger fish. I thought he was pulling my leg again so I ignored and soon forgot about it.. I then flopped over the side and descended to the sea bottom, which was only about 30 feet below.

I then looked around for fish but could not spot any. Then two parrot fish appeared from behind a rock and without thinking I speared one of them and took it back to the boat. Mike immediately recognised the fish and realised I'd speared one of his friends and told me so. I pleaded guilty to fish slaughter!

Geest Boats

On a different much bigger boat, Geest boats used to ply the islands regularly collecting bananas for shipment to Cardiff in Wales. They also played host to 12 paying guests who were wined and dined and were afforded the opportunity to visit all the islands when the boats docked to pick up bananas.

We were often invited on board to enjoy the hospitality and would trade beef (imported from the US) for items we could not get in Dominica such as English potatoes, beans and crisps.

On one such occasion a Roman party theme night was being held and dressed in togas and gowns we attended in glorious splendour to have a ball as the boat docked in Roseau. As the night progressed, I think I had too many rum cocktails and decided to become a stowaway or simply fell asleep somewhere on board.

Later I was shaken, awaken, and given cups of water and coffee as they carried and bundled me off the ship in Portsmouth - in the north of the island. It must have been a funny sight as I'm sure I was still wearing a toga. How we got home I still don't know to this day.

On-Board the British Navy

We would also be invited onto British naval ships when they called into port. The officers and crew would invite good looking girls and to be fair their partners. We would also entertain the crew and show them the island when they were allowed onshore.

Major Events

Carnival

J'Overt. Juve or Carnival

Carnival is two-day feasting event before Lent, which dates way back to European Roman Catholic Church history and was brought to the West Indies by the French settlers. In Dominica, this event formally known as Masquerade has a strong Afro- French influence. This all began when the French Aristocracy donned fancy, colorful masks and visited each other while their slaves danced and celebrated outdoors. Upon emancipation the then freed people began to celebrate in the streets. In its early form, carnival in Dominica was a group of people gathering to sing spontaneous songs accompanied by a musical band, a practice continued in a few villages to date. The Hi Fi and live bands on the road have replaced this practice in the city and bigger villages.

What is called the Jump Up or Street Party extends over the two-day period but there are many shows and activities, which precede this. Carnival in Dominica is officially launched with the opening of Carnival City at least one month before the official street Jump Up. This is an exciting and colorful afternoon of parades.

The Carnival Queen contestants, Calypsonians, Cheerleaders, Princess Show contestants, Sensay costumes and Darkies all parade the streets. This parade culminates in a small show where a number of the persons on parade perform on stage. The Street Jump Up always starts two days before Ash Wednesday.

The launching of carnival celebrations is followed by a series of activities and shows. There are numerous calypso shows held to determine the Calypso King each year.

Calypso is a style of Afro-Caribbean music which began in the days of slavery. The slaves robbed of their culture and homes used this as a way to communicate with each other and to mock the slave masters. Today Calypso is a musical art form in the Caribbean and is used as social commentary to criticize or praise governments or people on society and debate regional and international happenings.

The Carnival Queen Pageant, Teenage Pageant, and Princess show is also held in the days leading up to carnival. In these shows, the young women are judged in talent, beauty, intelligence, and their ability to carry a costume, which depicts Dominican carnival and culture. The Queen Pageant winner goes on to represent Dominica at regional and international beauty pageants.

As the years go by several shows have been added to the festivity. The Lapeau Kabwit/ Sensay festival is celebrated each year. This depicts a more traditional part of our carnival heritage. The Lapeau Kabwit (goatskin) is a band, which uses drums made up of goatskin, a tradition derived from their African ancestors.

These bands use several other instruments including a conch shell, Shak Shak, and of late horns have been added to make beautiful melodies and like in the days of slavery several of these bands have followers who sing songs composed on a whim.

The Sensay is a traditional costume depicting African heritage. This costume is made up of any material, which is available at the time: rope, straw, colorful cloth and is worn with a mask, which can portray an animal face, clown or the revelers face is simply painted. These are two aspects of carnival in Dominica which makes it truly original and unique when compared to carnival on the other islands in the Caribbean.

Over the years an International Artists Night has also been incorporated into the island's carnival festivities. On this night foreign bands are invited to perform. The most popular bands among Dominicans are the Soca bands that come from neighboring Caribbean countries. Soca music like Calypso, also originated in the Caribbean. It takes its roots in Calypso and Indian music and is not as serious as Calypso in terms of social commentary and was developed to get people dancing and sweating .

Perhaps the most anticipated element of Carnival in Dominica is the Street Jump Up. This begins early Monday morning about four o'clock (4:00 am) with what is called the J'Overt.

Traditionally people would dress up in pajamas or anything they could put their hands on at the time and rush to the streets to begin carnival. This is still practiced. Most people dress up in pajamas with bright colors and powder on their faces. Don't freak out if you see a young man dressed in his Grandmothers pajamas, it is carnival and anything goes. This normally ends about seven in the morning.

Monday morning Street Jump Up begins with a street parade at ten in the morning. Lots of costumed bands are on display and are judged based on how they move together and the brilliance and beauty of their costumes.

Each year bands compete for the coveted titles of King and Queen of the Band and Band of the Year among others. The beauty pageant contestants also parade in their costumes. It is truly a colorful and wonderful experience. Also parading are bands depicting traditional costumes and music. This ends by midday and about one in the afternoon people are back on the road again dancing to the sounds of music coming from huge trucks. The street party ends at eight at night.

The Jump Up continues on Tuesday with t-shirt bands which business institutions normally adopt and in which people wear t-shirts, which sometimes has a positive message printed. People are very reluctant to leave when the time to leave comes and often beg the bands to play longer. These two days of dance and festivities in the streets is phenomenal, everybody united to have a great, wild time gyrating to upbeat and moving music. Some sleeping where they lie.

Even if you are not a carnival lover, the sounds vibrating form the trucks make you move your feet. Carnival parades are held in Roseau, the capital and many villages on the island with Carnival Monday and Tuesday made public holidays in Dominica.

Ash Wednesday is a day of rest but the villages who follow the true carnival tradition continue on Wednesday with what is called the burning of Vaval. Vaval is the spirit of carnival and is made to resemble a huge doll. It is made up of rags, fibers, or any material the locals can put their hands on.

The Vaval is paraded through the village and burned at sunset to mark the ending of revelry and the beginning of Lent. This practice was brought to the islands by the French and at present is celebrated in the Carib Reserve and Dublanc.

Carnival in Dominica is said to be original since it has not been modernized much and still has most aspects of the traditional carnival celebrated during slavery. Many visitors and Dominicans living overseas flock to Dominica each year to take part in one of the Caribbean's most colourful and festive celebrations.

My fond memories are watching the street bands and processions pass by in the street from the comfort of a first floor balcony, to following behind one of the bands swaying to the rhythm and the beat to then see everyone before me jump over the walls of the church to make love in the grounds, to guys falling asleep in the streets to wake up the next day and start partying all over again fortified not just by Mountain Dew-80% proof rum - but also with goat stew cooked in oil drums, to the competitions for Carnival King and Queen, and colourful costumes and smiles to be seen everywhere - and above all everyone having fun..

Independence Day Celebrations

On 3rd November 1978 the Commonwealth of Dominica became independent from Britain with Patrick Roland John appointed as its first Prime Minister. There was a lot of preparation for the festivities all of which lasted a whole week and I was fortunate to be appointed as a government liaison officer, which meant that I went to them all. Sounded great.

Now, on and around every 3rd November, there are numerous celebrations and special events all over Dominica. For example, there are culture fests with food, song, and dance, a beauty pageant, a bullfight, a focus on the special heritage of a different village each year, outdoor markets, an emphasis on creole culture, and more including dancing, singing and merry making throughout the night. This is captured in a book of cartoons published by the New Chronicle.

The celebrations are so big, in fact, that 4 November has been designated Community Service Day in Dominica so the massive mess made on 3 November can be cleaned up!

From an historical perspective, Dominica was discovered by Christopher Columbus in 1493 and gained independence from Great Britain on the 3rd of November 1978. Since then Dominica has been self-governed and has a Democratic Parliamentary style of government.

As mentioned Dominica celebrates its independence each year with a series of festivals and celebrations. These festivities do not only celebrate the island's independence but serves as a means of reuniting the people living there to celebrate its history, traditions, cuisine and Creole culture.

The Independence celebrations in Dominica begin in September with a series of cultural competitions held in different districts on the Island. On display are numerous traditional dances, songs and folk story tellers locally called Kont. The dancers dress in traditional costumes, and dance to traditional music played by a small band which accompanies them onstage.

The traditional dress was inherited form African ancestors and reflects the outfits worn by free Creoles on market day, carnival and other festivities. The traditional dress includes the Wob Dwiyet and the Jupe worn by the women. This is accompanied by a headpiece called the Tete Case and a Foulard. The dresses are made up of madras or very colorful material. The men wear black trousers with white shirts, waist coats and a red sash around their waist.

The traditional musicians make sweet music using instruments such as the Accordion, Triangle, A local drum called the Tambou, Shak Shak, and the Boom Boom are all made from local natural materials. The folk dances performed at these competitions includes Quadrille, Mazook, Bele, Jing Ping, Heel and Toe and Flirtation, all of which are strongly influenced by our African and the Europeans who once colonized the island. The winners of the various districts all converge at a grand concert called the National Cultural Gala on the 4th of November each year.

In the months, leading up to Independence Day the country is alive with festivals. The National Folksong Festival which celebrates the talent of Dominicans and their abilities to put a story in song, which is a tradition developed by slaves to entertain themselves is held each year. Also occurring in October is the Heritage Day celebrations where one community is celebrated each year for its excellence and contributions toward the enhancement of the culture of the island.

As part of the Independence celebrations in Dominica each year a National Wob Dwiyet competition is held. As mentioned earlier the Wob Dwiyet is the National Dress of Dominican women. This exciting pageant judges the talents of the young women who participate and their ability to wear and carry the national dress.

A big part of the Independence celebrations is Creole Day. This is a celebration of the island's Creole heritage. On this day, people are encouraged to speak only French Creole and wear the national dress to work, school or just for a visit to town. For the entire day, French Creole is spoken on the radios and local television stations. This day is taken very seriously, and only local traditional food is prepared at homes, hotels, restaurants and bars.

These foods include, Green Bananas and Salt Fish, Callaloo, Mountain chicken, delicious crabs, Roast breadfruit and other local delicacies. It is held on the last Friday each October. The following day is Market Day which is celebrated at the main produce market, the Roseau Market where I worked. Again there is a carnival like atmosphere. On display are beautifully decorated market stalls where vendors sell local produce, craft and authentic local cuisine.

A new and much welcomed addition to the Independence celebrations in Dominica is Creole in the Park. This event started in 2003 and was organized by Cable and Wireless. It is a week-long celebration, which displays local talent and cuisine. This began as a need to provide entertainment for locals and visitors during the independence celebrations.

Perhaps what can be called Dominica's biggest festival to date, the World Creole Music Festival is celebrated during independence in Dominica. This festival spans over three nights and has been held the last weekend in October for the last eleven years. It displays local, regional and international artists and attracts visitors from around the globe to the shores of the Nature Isle.

National Flag Day and National Youth Parade is celebrated on 2 November. Nationals fly their flags proudly from their homes, business places and offices and from their vehicles. All schools from around the country verge in one place in a huge parade, where the students march and salute the Prime Minister of the country. Awards are also given out to those students and young persons who excel in academics, sports, culture and other aspects of society.

November the third is Independence Day. The day begins with a parade at the National Stadium where uniformed troops such as the Police and Firemen march and salute the Prime Minister. This is also a national holiday.

The independence celebrations end with a National Day of Community service each year. As the name suggests, people volunteer to work in their various communities. People take on projects and other activities, which help and aid their community. It is a day of fun and togetherness, while some work others prepare huge pots of food and it is broadcasted live on the local radio stations.

As time passes the Independence celebrations in Dominica pick up momentum with the addition of activities which reflects the country's cultural heritage and people.

Here are some of my highlights...

The Postage Stamps

By sheer co-incidence the guy I lodged with at school, Mick Wood, who worked for Waddingtons (Printers), designed the Independence Day Stamps but there was a lot of re-work that had to be done as Patrick John the Prime Minister wanted the colour of his face to be whitened (like Michael Jackson?).

Inspecting the Troops at the Airport

As an appointed Government Liaison Officer, I was invited to the official events. The first notable one was the arrival of Princess Margaret from the UK to Melville Hall Airport to inspect the troops on the tarmac after she landed. She was also the Royal representative who would officially hand over Independence to the Island.

She looked a little shaken if not stirred as she stepped off the plane. She then walked across and inspected the Dominican troops escorted by a British Army Officer. What she may not have known was that the British Officer who had been training the local troops had to step in at the last minute as the local Sargent Major who was supposed to be leading the inspection had to pull out at the last minute because he lost his voice !

The Official Handing-Over Ceremony

This took place in the evening and was held in the Cricket Ground. It was a splendid affair with a lot of pageantry followed by speeches and sworn oaths of Patrick John, the Prime Minister and newly appointed government officials. All was going smoothly to plan and few mistakes were made with the possible exception of the Minister of Finance forgetting to place his hand on the bible when being sworn in.

Then the grand finale, a firework display from atop the hills behind the stadium, which was being delivered by Pains-Wessex. All started well with fireworks filling the sky in a bright array of colour and sound but after about 20 seconds it fizzled out and died. No-one in the stadium knew why?

A few days later I met with the Manager of Pains–Wessex who gave me an explanation. As the firework display started one of the rocket stands fell over and set the surrounding grass alight. The local fire fighting force who were on hand leapt into action and doused and destroyed the whole display before it could get going.

Reception on HMS Juno

Princess Margaret kindly hosted a reception on board HMS Juno, which had arrived a few days earlier. She personally greeted and spoke to everyone except of course me who made a complete fool of myself. You see the Governor of the Island who was responsible for the invitations forget to invite me and my wife so I gate-crashed the party and told Princess Margaret. She was obviously not impressed. Suppose I was lucky I wasn't arrested, asked to walk the plank, thrown overboard, or shot!

Too Many Receptions

Receptions and Parties rolled on day and night for a whole week. On the last night, I think I had had enough drink to sink a battleship and ended up swimming on my balcony in the pouring rain. Unfortunately, I did not realise that the Landlord, who lives in Barbados, was back for the celebrations and was occupying the flat downstairs, until of course I heard him coughing. Well, that helped sober me up, shut up, get up and I staggered off to bed.

Civil Revolution

Patrick John, the Prime Minister, was implicated in a number of questionable dealings, including a scheme to lease land to a firm allegedly planning to supply petroleum illegally to South Africa, which was then under an international trade embargo because of its government's apartheid policy.

There were also rumors that the Northern region of the island, which possesses the richest farmland, was going to be leased for a $1 an acre to the Mafia in Miami.

Subsequently, the Civil Service went on strike and demonstrations were held outside government buildings. Even gunshots were heard one day as potential riots were dispersed. This was on a day when my wife had gone hiking in the mountains with a girlfriend whilst I spent time with UK government staff trying to find out what was going on. Everyone was worried. Expats went to ground. That said it all quietened down quickly and my wife returned safe and sound without a clue as to what had been going on

Nonetheless a Cabinet crisis ensued, and in May 1979 Oliver Seraphine emerged as the new Prime Minister.

Hurricane David

The Facts

It is a date that is etched in the minds of many Dominicans: August 29, 1979. It was the day Hurricane David struck Dominica. It is a day etched in mine.

Hurricane David severely damaged the island. The storm not only largely destroyed the banana crop, the island's economic mainstay, but it also carried away most of the island's topsoil and virtually wiped out the country's agricultural base. The following year, Hurricane Allen set the economy back further.

The island had only twice been previously struck by a severe hurricane. In a hurricane in 1806, 131 people died when the Roseau River shifted its course and flooded the capital. On September 10, 1834, 200 lives were lost as a result of what was to be known as the 'Great Hurricane.'

In addition, in 1979 Hurricane David, a Category 5 hurricane and one of the deadliest of the latter half of the 20th century, roared towards the island.

Days before, forecasters predicted the hurricane would spare Dominica and hit Barbados instead. However, hours before moving closer to the islands the hurricane shifted and headed for Dominica. Although it was clear David was coming, residents did not appear to take the situation seriously.

Hence, the island was very unprepared as there was little local radio warning and no systems in place for disaster preparedness. Packing winds of 150 miles-per-hour the hurricane pounded Dominica for six hours from 9:00 am.

Thirty-seven people were killed and an estimated 5,000 were injured. Three-quarters of the population of 75,000 were left homeless. Many people slept in the open or huddled in homes of fortunate friends and neighbors for weeks or months to come.

My Experience

My experience of the hurricane is summed up in a poem that I wrote:

Hurricane David
Dominica 1979

Early dawn
Not much, sleep as we await our fate
Listening to the radio
For any news
Of the flight of a hurricane
That lies in our wake.

Hurricane passing us to the South
Then turned its eye north towards our island
Local Radio Station went off the air
Only 2 hours' notice to get to safety
In the confines of a hurricane proof shelter
Not been used for years.

So off we go to L Rose & Co
A mansion set in an unspoilt estate of pristine palm trees
Deep down, nested in the valley below
That is where we are heading
Fate unknown.

We arrive at 7.30 am
3 couples, our 2 dogs and the resident's cat
In the kitchen having a rum and coke or mebbe a beer
Locked in, a sense of excitement, as well as fear.

Outside, flocks of birds take flight

As winds rise, trees start to sway
Animals lie down, seemingly calm, sitting tight.

The noise becomes deafening
Doors and shutters rattle
We stand firm in the kitchen
Ready and waiting for the ensuing battle.

No-one moving,
Mebbe a slight tinkle and tremble
Of a glass as the rum goes down
Welcome relief when faced with danger
No one knows what's coming
But a sense of comfort
We are not alone
We are all together.

Then a vast rumbling noise
Followed by a whooshing sound
Bolts popping, tin screaming,
It's a hell of a din
As the roof lifts, off.
Glasses shaking
However, we are still stood firm on the ground.
Utensils, pots and pans sucked up into the void
Spinning, swirling within a tornado
Rising up then suddenly gone
And disappearing.

As if in a warp drive
Here one moment, then zapped into the air
Ain't no Fairground, more a melee in a Merry-go-round.
Did I see Dorothy in the Wizard of Oz fly by?

In a house flying across the sky?
Unfortunately, no this is not a film
It's real, threatening and frightening
We're facing death in this cold chilling morn.

No time to contemplate or live in a dream
This is a nightmare, the worst I've seen
Time to run, move on
So off we go
And rush into another room.

We evacuate to the lounge
We lock the door
And crouch behind on the polished floor
But the door starts to creak, buckle and bend
We shove antique furniture against it
But can see light emerging through the hinges and frame
So, without thought or feelings of shame
And nothing but ourselves to defend
We start breaking the legs off the furniture
And nail them to the moving door and buckled frame.

Lounge roof then lifts off, along with the door
We run to the back of the house to a small bedroom
And wait huddled, quiet, listening for more.

We place the cat on top of the wardrobe
While the dogs sit expectantly and like us retain a constant stare
At the cat and the roof, hoping they won't disappear

Well not to be disappointed
Off they go, the roof and door, to join their friends
I sit a Merry-go-Round or Hell in a Den.

The wardrobe stands, but rocking and swinging with the cat
Gripping tightly with its claws as if death is waiting at the door
I tell my friends to leave as I try rescue him
But then, clutching the cat, rafters fall driving us both to the floor.

Friends return and provide a welcome hand
I'm rattled and stirred, cat is petrified
But glad to still be around
Limbs not broken just our pride as dust and rum clears from my head
And the cat is happy with feet back firmly on the ground.

We go to the balcony
Which has wire netting all around
And surround ourselves with tables and mattresses
And anything within reach
That will keep us safe and sound.

Then the nightmare returns
The evil wind whips up again
And peels back the balcony roof like a banana
That is stripped, yellow and bears no shame.

We dive over the balcony
Like mariners deserting a sinking ship
Bottle and animals in hand
We crawl underneath.

Then total silence
No sound outside.

Taking breath
We emerge into the open air
Now surrounded by a circulating white wall of death

I look up into the funnel towards the sky
Clear blue, and yet seemingly passing us by.
We are in the Eye.

In the Eye of the Storm
Surreal and temporarily safe
But it's moving slowly towards us
Across the estate
I realise it will hit us again
But from the other direction
At no stopping this one
To hell we are bound.

So back we go
Reinforce the cramped space that we know
To sit it out under the balcony
With determination and resolve.

Come hell and high water
And the persistent wind and rain
We survived it once
We will survive it again.

When it's all over
The sun again shines
Life returns to normal
And everything is just fine.

Yes it was a frightening experience though I always thought we would get through it come hell or high water.

After the hurricane, I looked out to see the driveway covered by Royal Palms that had fallen across its path and the double garage blown out yet not a scratch on my insured car. That said I could not drive it out as the road was blocked.

Seeing the devastation, I decided I had better walk back to our rented house to see what damage had been done. The shortest route was up a cliff road but half way up it was also blocked by trees some over 200 feet in length. I noticed that one reached to the top of the cliff so I climbed up it. Near the top, I heard a rustling noise and the tree became unsteady, then it slipped then thundered down the cliff as I hung-on by fingertips to the top of the cliff. I prayed then clambered up over the top.

I stopped and got my breath back, looked around and took in the devastation in front and all around me. Most of the houses had lost their roofs, including ours. To get to it I had to walk through the ruins of someone else's house, as there was no way round it. The next day I was to learn that people had died in that house.

Once through the debris of the house I climbed up the small hill to our house, up the stairs to the first-floor entrance and entered with my key to find up to a foot of water and bat excrement on the floor. Most of the roof had gone and all the bats that lived in the roof had flown.

I tried to sweep all the water and mess out of the doors but realised then that the floors were not level and the brackish water was deeper in the bedrooms. So I went into the yard, got a pickaxe and knocked holes in the wall to let the bracken water out.

Once the water had drained I surveyed the place. Everything was a mess and with hardly any roof I realised we could not stay there. So, I returned to the L Rose estate, gave my thanks and said my goodbyes to the hosts who were packing to go find a hotel, whilst my wife, dogs and I walked and took the long way round to our house. I then broke a window on the downstairs flat entered and we stayed there until the end of my contract.

The next day I went to our office, the wooden shack in the Botanical Gardens to find that it had also been broken into and looted. On the way back I was walking across a playing field when two helicopters appeared and landed, one was a British navy helicopter, I think it was a Westland, and the other American, a Sikorsky, that I later learned was nicknamed "The Jolly Green Giant".

About 10 soldiers and engineers jumped out and I was approached by both captains who asked me about the dam that fed water to the town. They explained that they had been told it was blocked and they had come to clear it but needed transport as the helicopters had been assigned to other important rescue duties. I led them to a garage where I requisitioned a truck and petrol and then led them up into the hills out of town to the dam.

On the way, I stopped at my friends, Carol and Alans place, to check if Carol and the dogs were ok as Alan was on a trip to the States. She was fine so we carried on to the dam clearing the road of debris and fallen trees as we went... I spent the day helping the people manually clear the dam until a civil servant approached me and told me I was required at a government meeting. How he knew I was at the dam, I don't know. I just had time to eat some navy rations that consisted mainly of corn beef and mash and was then rushed off to the government building in Roseau.

I got into the meeting to find all the Ministers there and representatives from the UNDR, French US and British Governments. After some discussion of the state of the emergency and emerging issues they started to go round the table and assign tasks. I was beginning to wonder why I was there when I was asked to confirm that I was training to be a Management Accountant and had done some accounts and plans for the Marketing Board, which I acknowledged.

I was getting even more curious and wondering where all this was leading to when out of the blue I was asked to set up accounting records for monitoring food aid and relief supplies that were to be sent and stored in district warehouses and managed by local Councils.

So next day I designed a simple itemised stock in/stock out system on paper and was rather pleased with myself until it dawned on me that I could not circulate or distribute it.as roads were blocked and telecoms were down.

I raised this issue with the Permanent Secretary and we then managed to get hold of a Bell helicopter with a volunteer Venezuelan crew of 6 cowboys who were equipped with ham radios.

I spent the next couple of days flying around jumping out of the helicopter and setting these guys up in the districts so that we eventually established an island-wide radio network. I then spent my time co-ordinating efforts to get supplies from Melville Airport which had been taken over by the Seebees (US Navy Construction Engineers) and supplies coming into the ports in Roseau and Portsmouth.

I also established air control in the Canefield airstrip which was being built near Roseau to allow short take-off and landing aircraft to come in which also allowed other agencies like the Crown Agents and relief agencies to ferry urgent supplies from neighbouring islands that were least affected.

Then, excusing the pun the service took off. I got involved in organising the ferrying of injured or seriously ill people and pregnant women to hospital, providing an emergency help line and messaging service, moving medical supplies where urgently needed, and averting looting.

On a lighter note, I came across one woman carrying what she thought was a TV from a shop, who wasn't too happy when I told her it was a washing machine.

Whilst acknowledging the tremendous instantaneous support and sterling work carried out by aid agencies and governments from many different countries, the British Development Division inadvertently ordered one thousand portable loos and several thousand chain saws that turned out to be no better than hedge trimmers. Needless to say, this order was cancelled.

In the absence of electricity for 6 weeks after the hurricane, the airstrip service for the Crown Agents turned out to be useful, as they would kindly fly in a crate of ice, which we would throw beers into to cool down. Of course, it meant we had to finish them all off before the ice melted.

The Venezuelan team also gave me a t-shirt, which had Venezuela written on it in different colours on a white background, which I gave to my wife, for me to find out later that they were giving them to all the women they had met. Whilst providing a critical service they were clearly enjoying themselves and being treated locally like VIPs.

Then it all stopped. I was called in by the Permanent Secretary to be told that whilst we had done a great job it was now to be handed over to the police and local officials, I was to return to my job in agriculture and the team was to return to Venezuela.

Well, I guess all good things must come to an end.

Coming Home

It wasn't long before the end of my contract and we had to prepare to go home. I was to receive a bonus, which I wanted to spend travelling around South America whilst my wife wanted to take the dogs home.

This wasn't an easy decision as we could find no-one to take them in and we didn't want to let the dogs run wild, and wouldn't consider putting them down. So, we decided to get them home and before us as they would have to face six months quarantine.

Getting them home wasn't as easy as it sounds. We had to make crates for them and take them to Antigua by fishing boat overnight

We departed from Roseau docks in a beat up old smelly fishing boat. Surprisingly many of our friends turned up to see us and the dogs off and we had a few beers to cheer us on our merry way. We were still shouting goodbyes as the boat dropped its moorings and moved slowly out from the jetty whereupon I, in a somewhat exuberant gung-ho spirit, threw my empty bottle to Richard my friend on the jetty. Unfortunately, he caught it whilst still holding his bottle of beer in his hand. They collided and broke and beer sprayed all over him. Fortunately, he was not cut and to this day I regret doing it and realising how foolish I had been.

Whilst the fishing boat was old and smelly, surprisingly, we left the dogs above board in the cool night breeze whilst we slept in a small rotting cabin next to the engine room.

Sleep was not easy and made worse by the fact that Buster our little dog managed to bite his way out of his cage and broke a tooth in doing so. We woke to a lot of barking and commotion up top. I rushed up the stairs to the deck to see Buster running round the boat and the crew unable to catch him. Reminded me of a Snowy and Tin - Tin sketch

When Buster saw me he wagged his tail, calmed down and came to me. I saw blood coming from his mouth so checked it. The broken tooth didn't look too bad so reckoned he could make the rest of the trip home without treatment.

It was early morning and the sun was coming up so we put both dogs on their leads and sat on the bow of the boat until we entered Castries harbour in St Lucia.

Once through a rudimentary Customs check we enquired where we could get Buster's kennel fixed and were soon on our way in a big white taxi with blue number plates to a Carpenter's shop outside town where he replaced the wire and hinges on the door.

With only a few hours to go we then went to the Airport where the dogs' paperwork was checked and a vet administered a mild sedative to the dogs to make their passage easier. With tears in our eyes but hope in our hearts we said our temporary goodbyes to the dogs and got flights back to Dominica.

We, or should I say I, then seemed to spend a month packing a large crate to take home. We didn't have much stuff but managed to fill a 8X 4X 4 foot crate, fortified by rafters off the roof, which had fallen during the hurricane.

When finished packing Mike the ex-Navy diver came round and asked if he could have my snorkelling gear and weights but unfortunately it was packed at the bottom of the crate and I wasn't going to unpack it all. Noticing though that there was some room on the top, he asked if we could take some stuff back for his family. I thought nothing of it until he turned up with two large turtle shells. Needless to say, they were confiscated by Customs when they arrived later by sea freight in Barry in Wales.

In the few days before we left we said goodbye to so many friends we had made. It was sad.

On final departure, we went to Melville Hall Airport on the other side of the island. We went alone and no one came to see us off, as it was a long journey over rugged roads and mountains. At the airport, everything went smoothly until we landed in Barbados to get a connecting flight. Upon attempting to board the plane I was told that my briefcase had to go into the hold. Reluctantly I allowed this to happen though all my education certificates, pictures of the hurricane, driving licence etc were contained within it. That was the last I saw of it. Back in the UK, it took me months to replace it all.

Quarantine in Folly Foot Kennels

Our two dogs were placed in Folly Foot kennels in Panel near Harrogate in Yorkshire not far from where the in-laws lived. The place was like something out of the TV series Heartbeat or Tales of The Summer Wine.

The dogs were getting 5-star treatment yet struggling with the gourmet food which consisted of tins of dog meat. Not being used to eating tins of dog meat, they initially refused to eat it. We got a call from the in-laws saying that the kennel wanted to know what they ate. Well, as mentioned they used to eat rice with anything thrown in or left over. This got lost in translation so the kennels fed them tins of milk pudding, which surprisingly they got used to.

At visiting-time the kennels would ring a bell and just like a Pavlov response where dogs would identify and relate sound to specific events, the dogs would get excited. Buster being small had to jump several feet to see out of his cage, which I guess, was funny to see.

When they were eventually released after quarantine, they were brought to the in-laws house and immediately went up to a rubber plant and peed on it. This was topped by an incident whereupon the in-laws were out and their budgerigar was flying from its cage to the top of the pelmet on a window curtain. This didn't last long as Bruce took and dispatched it in mid-flight. So. it took a while for the dogs to acclimatise and adjust to a new way of living but they both lived to a grand old age of 15 years whereas the life span of a dog in Dominica was typically about 7 years.

Epilogue

Whilst I had a great experience and thoroughly enjoyed myself in Dominica, at the time I thought a career as an Economist wasn't a particularly safe one so in a sense I was determined to return to the UK and obtain a qualification as a Management Accountant for which I had done some preparation.

From a career point of view, this was a wise decision but when I look back, I miss those days and miss the work I subsequently did in overseas development. Indeed, had I been single I think it would have been a different journey and a different story.

My wife and I stayed at the in-laws for several months whilst I fixed the beat-up Hilman Avenger that I had returned from Dominica. This was done out in the drive

during Winter. To this day, I do not know how I managed to do it. Indeed, when we got back to the UK. I can remember being so cold and sitting in front of the fire to defrost my feet, when my socks caught alight!

I also sat the first level of the Management Accounting qualification and failed. That said I then flew through all the stages in 18 months and passed with flying colours. This put me in good stead and enabled me to obtain rapid promotions firstly working for Grand Met, then Price Waterhouse Coopers, in London.

After working for PWC for several years, I was approached by US Aid to work in the Prime Minister's Office in Dominica. Being career and family focused I turned it down. Later I found out that Carol Bunting our dear American friend was Secretary to Eugena Charles the PM. To this day I so regret those decisions

....

And so, I end this book with gratitude and thanks for the experience of a lifetime.

One day I will return.

One day I will relive the fond memories, renew old friendships and make new friends.

I look forward to the next Chapter, and thank you for reading this.

....

Dave was born and grew up on the shores of England and following his schooling traveled around the World working for consultancies and institutions like PWC, the World Bank and the United Nations, in some of the richest and indeed poorest places on the planet.

Besides troubleshooting projects, sometimes in the middle of nowhere, sometimes left on his own, he learned much about people and life, its challenges and experiences, some deep and profound. His writing started with poetry about life, love, travel and disasters, and grew over time as he kept pinching himself to write this book about his exploits and experience in Dominica.

An experience, which he will never forgot and which will stay with him forever.

Printed in the United States
by Baker & Taylor Publisher Services